WOMEN WITH WINGS

Hand in Hand & Heart to Heart

Songbook

WOMEN WITH WINGS

Hand in Hand & Heart to Heart
Songbook

www.susanwilsonphoto.com

This songbook is dedicated to
Kay Louise Gardner
February 8, 1941 - August 28, 2002

Hand in Hand & Heart to Heart
Original Chants and Songs of Affirmation and Empowerment
by
Women With Wings, 120 Park St., Bangor, ME 04401

Twenty of the songs in this songbook have been recorded by Women With Wings
and are available on the Hand in Hand & Heart to Heart CD
from the following resources
www.womenwithwings.org
www.ladyslipper.org
www.cdbaby.com

Front cover Art by Jami Cass
CD cover Art by Anne Tatgenhorst
Music notation by Kay Gardner and Linda J. Smith Koehler
Songbook coordinator Mida Ballard
Book design by Kim Hawkins

Third revised edition March 2010

For information and ordering contact: womenwithwingsbangor@gmail.com
or see our website: www.womenwithwings.org

For bulk commercial orders contact:

Quiet Waters Publications
P.O. Box 34
Bolivar, MO 65613-0034
E-mail: QWP@usa.net

ISBN 1-931475-28-8

Library of Congress Control Number: 2005906051

Table of Contents

Songs of Affirmation

Mother Earth Songs

Goddess Songs

Moon Songs

Healing Songs

Songs for Rituals

Indexes

Notes:
* Song titles in bold are recorded on the CD Hand in Hand & Heart to Heart
** Songs by Ina (ee-na) were originally copyrighted under the
   name Ana K.W. Moffet
*** Songs by Jami Cass were originally copyrighted under the name
   Jami Herring Bradshaw

Our Purpose Statement: We seek the spiritual empowerment of women. It is our goal to create safe, sacred space for exploring women's spirituality through music. Through song we intend to enhance consciousness of Mother Earth, express love for the environment, and celebrate traditions from many cultures. As we find the power behind our voices, we then blend that power to create an even greater voice

Photo by Sue Fitzgerald

For many years while touring as a composer of healing music and a teacher of the curative properties of music, folks would ask me if I had a sound healing practice at home. Until 1993, the year Women With Wings began, I had to say "no," but Wings has become my practice. And it's not just my own practice, it is a practice for every individual woman within the circle, and it is even more. It has become a group healing practice.

What could be more magic and more healing than singing in a community of sisters? Our grandmothers sang while they quilted together. As we did when young, our daughters sing around summer campfires. Every week Women With Wings—a circle of women ages eight to eighty—meet in a huge resonant room, the vestry of the Unitarian Universalist Church in Bangor, Maine. We always start our two-hour singing circle with this song:
> There's a river of birds in migration
> A nation of women with wings

When we began, in '93, we sang songs and chants and rounds gathered from many diverse sources: from recordings, from workshops and festivals attended by our members, from various spiritual traditions, and from ceremonial gatherings with our friends. After our evenings of singing together we felt radiant and whole. We realized that singing words of affirmation and empowerment were like healing prayers, and that not only did the music carry the prayers out to the universe, but they resounded within our deepest souls as well. As the years passed and each woman's voice grew stronger and surer, original chants – affirmations with tunes – began flowing like streams from many of us, mostly women who had never created music in their lives. These chants were birthed organically while driving to and from work, while praying, while doing housework, or while observing Nature's miracles. Some even arose spontaneously while in the circle itself!

Within our circle are women on many different life paths. We are single, married, straight, lesbian, professional women, tradeswomen, teachers, homemakers, and young, old, able in body and mind, challenged in body and mind. We are mothers, aunts, and grandmothers bringing our lives and loves to the circle every week, creating a light-filled spiritual energy that we are convinced, because it has changed us, can change the world.

Each of dozens of songs in this songbook came as a gift. Each song is offered as a gift, not only to our women's community-at-large, but to the world community of women, men and children. May we all be united in song, and may our shared songs help to bring more peace and love to the world.

Kay Gardner
July 4, 2002

DEDICATION

KAY LOUISE GARDNER
February 8, 1941 – August 28, 2002

A woman of physical and spiritual beauty and immense musical talent
A woman of courage and vision for radical change
A woman of passion and will, creativity and humor
An intellectual, a composer, a priestess, a mother

She became our leader – our mentor – our sister – and our friend
helping us to find our voices and our power
She is the point of light at the source of our spiral
She lives in the harmonies we sing and the healing energy we raise

And always and forever, her music helps us find our way home

Kay gave us the musical and spiritual support upon which to build our sacred singing circle, Women With Wings. From the beginning it was obvious that we would not be a traditional women's chorus but a flexible, fluid singing circle with spiritual healing and expression as its loving intent. Kay had the vision and courage to move beyond her sophisticated world of classical music to the transformational simplicity of chants and songs that are accessible to everyone. She loved working with those who loved to sing – trained or untrained – and taught us how to create a sacred space where every woman could find her voice and affirm her personal power.

Although she had recorded many CD's and toured extensively, Kay was content to be part of the informal, ever-changing group of women meeting in the vestry of the Unitarian Universalist Church in Bangor, Maine each Thursday evening. She encouraged us, prodded us, challenged us and wrote music for us. But most of all she loved us and let herself be loved by us as we became the local musical community that she had longed for. Some misunderstood and assumed that Women With Wings was Kay Gardner but she, herself, knew that she was there to plant a seed and nurture a new way of experiencing music as medicine before she had to move on to a new project or musical dimension.

Kay's gift was envisioning the impact of the healing energy of sound vibrations and loving intent created by circles of women singing and dancing the cycles of their lives. She held us until we could see ourselves as singers and songwriters, dancers and healers, and then, tired, she stepped back so that we could continue her work of encouraging women to heal themselves by doing something as natural as singing simple, life-affirming chants and melodies. She was the spark and Women With Wings is the flame.

May our music warm your heart and melt your sorrows so that your pain flows away and there is room for new life and spirit to blossom. May you experience the miraculous change that comes from hearing the sound of your voice singing the songs of your life echoed by women doing the same. May you come into our circle and sing with us and may we give thanks for spiritual teachers like Kay who come to open the door of new beginnings and re-memberings so that we can take our places in a circle that never ends.

Colleen Fitzgerald   January 2005

"I met Kay Gardner in the most unlikely of places, at just the right time in my life, before the group even had a name. I remember that first gathering, easing my way into a group of strangers in that Bangor church basement. The minute we formed a circle and opened our throats together, Women With Wings was born. This group and this music opened windows for me that I hadn't known were there. May WWW always soar."
           Lynn Flewelling

"I met Kay at the Hersey retreat, which was the inception of Wings. At the table, Coco was the one who suggested that we have a women's singing circle. When Kay said she thought that was a good idea and that we should meet once a week, I said, 'I can't fit that into my schedule. What about once a month?' Kay said it would never fly if it met once a month. I went for five years straight every week missing only a handful.

"Wings was a lifeboat for me. I was getting a divorce at the time and I truly felt that Wings put a rudder on my boat, which could tend to drift off course amidst the chaos of my life. The intention, integrity, safety, and support were an absolute lifeline to me.

"Kay's impeccable clarity of purpose around her music and music in general was pivotal for me to witness. She was an incredible role model for music as a healing medium, for singing to be what the person needed to get out of it, and for living her passion (not always easily but truly!). She was the first professional musician I met who did not involve her ego with the performance or the music. She worked for the purpose, not her own self-aggrandizement. It was quite a revelation to me at the time. She created a totally safe circle for each person to do her work and, for that, I will be eternally grateful. She was a mentor to me, and she probably never knew it. I do not think I am alone in this feeling. And besides all that, she liked to have fun!"
           Lee Cummings

"I will never forget Kay's generosity of spirit. I had been singing at Wings only four weeks when we were scheduled to sing at the Arts Festival in Brunswick. 'Regulars only,' said Kay. When I asked Kay about joining them for the event, her response was immediate: 'Four weeks? Of course. You're a regular.'

"Kay constantly reminds us to 'have fun' at concerts. No matter how many times we perform in public, most of us get at least a little anxious just before going on. At the end of warm up, Kay always says to us: 'And what do we need to remember?' The response from all of us: 'To have fun!' And we do.

"Through Kay's directorship, many of us have had the willingness and courage to explore our own musical creativity: writing songs, exploring new harmonies, expanding the range of comfort for our own individual voices (imagine my surprise to discover I was a soprano!), and not to feel injured when a particular foray was not successful."
           Anon.

"In remembrance of Kay…
I am eternally grateful to have been in Kay's presence and have shared in her awesome gifts. I honor you, Blessed Sister." **Mary Ellen Quinn**

"I remember Kay Gardner as a wise, loving, pioneering spirit, a very creative, talented musician, sound healer, teacher and author. She inspired me with her ability to tune in, experiment and create new musical forms, as well as to synthesize information from many sources and spiritual paths in her teachings and writings. She was a powerful woman, very human, generous and humble, who knew well how to support and empower others. She accomplished a great deal in her lifetime and left us a tremendous legacy. She will be deeply missed……" **Kate Marks**

NOT A WORD

I sit on a perfect granite seat
surrounded by brilliant blues
nose to the wind
like the gulls on rockweed below,
waiting for revelation at turn of tide.
No metaphor comes,
no neat turn of phrase,
not a word.

Rocks, wind, sun and surf
speak for themselves:
an elementary language
requiring no translation.
I watch a lone sail
ride over the earth's watery curve.
I sing her away with a single,
sustained note.

Maryann Ingalls
August 31, 2002
For Kay Gardner

Sharing What Women With Wings Means to Us

"When I started to sing with Wings, I felt it was like coming home. There are no auditions (judgments) or competitive vocalists. We sing by listening…no paper to study. Standing in the circle, I feel an acceptance and openness to creativity. This is where it happens.

"It is also a wonderful way to connect with a community of women. I knew no one when I first arrived. Now I see a Winger almost everywhere I go. Some have gone, some return occasionally, others are there every week. The women encompass a full range of humanness. That is, there are those who are strong leaders, those in need of healing and many personalities involved. We have laughed, cried, disagreed, and hugged, but it is the music that we come back to, and that is what keeps us together. The music is healing and that is why we are strong."   **Grace Walker**

"When I first heard Deb Christo's song, 'Be Here Now' in circle, I was deeply touched by its poignant simplicity. Later, as I watched my world fall apart around me, this song played an important part in my healing. I found myself spending time on a beach in Florida. As I wrestled with thoughts of impending gloom, Deb's song would come to me from across the sea. 'Be Here Now,' That concept to be here now would fill my head until I was forced to actually be here now and look around. Palm trees, a golden beach, crisp blue skies, surfers, and those tiny birds that endlessly race the tide. I was safe. It was only change. Be here now. This song kept me in the present, protecting me from my errant mind. An important teaching song came through Deb, a song teaching ancient, yet familiar wisdom. A song reminding each of us to 'Be Here Now,' to look around, to enjoy the gift that is life.

"Woman With Wings is a circle of voices that ebb and flow. Music, singing, circle energy lives deep inside each woman. The circle is a powerful tool, an ancient energy source for rebirth and regeneration. Creating sacred space, we allow primordial and ancient memories to surface. We women know these harmonies. We all know these rhythms. Lullabies, power songs, songs to lament, we sing these songs. We create these songs. We are Women With Wings. As songs are passed from mother to daughter and woman to woman, we give each other and ourselves the power of the circle."   **Robin Fre**

"Women With Wings has brought me through a threshold from my separate womanness into a collective experience of women. This is a place where I can show up, speak out, give and receive love and, of course, sing! To me Women With Wings is about belonging."
                    Crone Judith Coscarelli age 63

"I have had such a struggle with organized religion. On the one hand, I love my church and my church community. On the other hand, I find much of church teaching very painful. Women With Wings has provided me a spiritual, feminine counterweight that has allowed me to remain a member of my church, holding the tensions of belief and unbelief in some sort of creative imbalance.

"This circle of women has provided me spiritual health primarily. But, for the first two years I sang with Women With Wings, I had no illness, not even a cold. Apparently, singing here was a tremendous boost to my physical immune system.

"I will never forget the first time we sang Libby Roderick's 'How Can Anyone Ever Tell You' in public. Some women started to cry. Something in them needed to hear how beautiful they were, how complete. Subsequently, I saw others cry, one was a man. He needed to hear the same message.

"Most of us Wingers are very nervous about singing at first. Few of us have had any formal music education. Many of us believe we cannot sing. I will always remember the absolute terror the first time I sang my name during weekly introductions. Some of us really do have difficulty carrying a tune, but you know, we all sure can sing.

"The songs we sing often are spiritual and emotional affirmations of our worth, of the worth of others, of the divine in all things and in all places. They are prayers repeated over and over, week in and week out. We begin to believe them, and then we begin to live them."

Maryann Ingalls

"Being part of Women With Wings has been an affirming and empowering experience for me. Nine years ago, at a women's retreat, which 'birthed' this circle of song, and where I first met Kay Gardner, I learned that there was such a thing as women's music and that age and experience were positive things to be honored in rituals. The first song she taught us was, 'We are the old women, we are the new women, we are the same women, stronger than before!' How healing, for me to hear and feel these words/sounds after years of depression from the end of a thirty-eight year marriage. Since that day, I have not only been comforted and strengthened by my participation in Wings but have gained enough confidence to sing for/with hospice patients; it is supremely satisfying to see terminally ill people's faces relax when beautiful healing words are sung. First I received comfort and now I can give comfort to others. The circle of love continues and grows."

Carolyn Kinnard Ziffer   Age 70

My Dear Winged Sister-Friends:

"The simple truth is…without you, I would not have learned to fly, to soar (higher and higher), to rise and ride a thermal, to see the distant horizon – rather than just the path below. Your wings helped me to remain aloft when my own were too heavy – laden with sadness and loss.

"You have each, in turn, embraced me with the warmth of your hugs and kisses, kept me safe within the folds of the flock. When I could not see through my tears, I listened for my heartbeat and found you in song. I have drunk from your wells of Love and Friendship, Beauty and Peace, Laughter and Mirth, and am once again uplifted, energized, FREE!

"I praise you. I love you. You are Goddesses all. Thank you for the Blessings of your unique Friendship. In Sisterhood and With Love, "   **Sandy Imondi**

"I turned on to the interstate for a twelve-hour trip south in the February snow. 'Beauty' began playing in my head. I listened, I sang. I noticed the beauty around me as the snow plowed trail I followed led me by pines, out croppings of rocks, fields and sleepy houses all covered with a cloak of soft white. Two hours into the drive the snow turned to rain. No white knuckled anxiety for me this trip. Just beauty and peace. We sing our songs for circle and life. Thanks, Grace.

"The hectic life of self-imposed responsibility with details, decisions and deadlines can be overwhelming. Beginning my day with a mental list of all I think I need to do before bedtime can zap my energy before I even begin. 'Be Here Now' turns frantic into calm and reminds me to notice my breath and to love. Debbie's is a song for all occasions."   **Alice**

"My journey with Wings began about five years ago. I attended a fall concert which featured, among many other wonderful songs, the complicated piece 'Root Women.' Being in the midst of my life path as an herbalist, this song struck deeply into me. I cried in agreement to 'I am the elephant, I am the bear.' This was the second time for hearing 'The Beautiful Song' and certainly the most beautiful rendition. My mind was made up immediately – I wanted to sing with these women! Ever since then I've traveled thirty-five miles each way most Thursdays to be a part of this ever-changing group. Several of us carpool and we sing at every concert and performance possible. Women With Wings has been a sacred, healing place where I have felt safe enough to find my voice. Wings' songs find their way into all parts of my life – from driving in the car, to rituals, celebrations, and the classes I teach. Now it's OK that I have a deep, loud voice. At Women With Wings, there's room for Nightingales as well as Frogs. Blessed be."   **Rani Lynn   June 27, 2002**

"Singing in circle fills my heart with joy! The amazing blend of our voices, joined as one, to celebrate, to comfort, to heal, to pray is a gift from God/Goddess. We are truly sisters, diverse and connected, on a journey discovering the Divine in each of us, through our songs."

Mary Ellen Quinn

"Thursday evenings are often a refuge and a surge of strength. Two hours of simple, repetitive songs that feed the soul ('My Spirit Lives On'), that tell me we are all divine and all can be sacred ('The Goddess Is In Me' and 'Holy Ground'), that comfort me ('Everything Will Be All Right'), that remind me to live in this moment ('Be Here Now'). Songs that are written by the women in Wings. Songs that are brought from other places in the world. Songs that are sung alone. Songs that are sung with others. Songs that remind me what life is about. "

Jan Silbury

"In the early days of Women With Wings, I actually felt myself coming back to life as if returning to consciousness after a long sleep. I let the colors and healing vibrations of the circle wash over me and peel back the layers of defensiveness that had grown from a lifetime of denying my inner beauty and not listening to my heart. The women who sang in circle gave me the courage, support, and acceptance that I needed to stop running from the power and creativity that are given to every woman at birth."

Colleen Fitzgerald

THIS LIFE SO FAR
(to my dearest friend)

I have been through many lives in this lifetime,
I am the new woman, I am the old woman, I am the eternal woman,
Life is full of lessons, not events
At almost 60, I am eager for my next lesson, however painful or challenging.
They all lead me to freedom,
Freedom for my spirit, satisfaction for my soul.
As I am freed from my past hurts, my ability to love and be loved increases.
With each day, I let you in, I let me out.
Freedom, Freedom,
Freedom in this life,
Freedom in my next life.

Cathy Baker

HEAR A SONG

Hear a song
Trust your heart
Sing it out loud

See a hand
Accept a gift
With thanks

Hear a cry
Offer your arms
For comfort

Sing a song
Feel the power
We share

Rosemarie Di Lernia

Sharing Excepts from Letters

"Randomly, I wandered…by a different route that took me past your door. Indulging my curiosity out of my feeling of emptiness and surrender, I decided to investigate the heavenly sounds I heard. When I saw the altar and the circle of women, I recognized part of my spirituality I had dropped and neglected as I entered my trials this past year. I was just going to watch from the shadows, but you welcomed me in. I sang my pain and joy with you and seemed to magically know all the words." **Catherine E., Stamford, CT**

"When you were singing at the Fair and invited the audience to come into our circle, I came into the circle and was glad that I did even though it was difficult for me because I don't sing. Because of childhood experiences, I have not been able to convince myself that it's okay to sing…One goal of mine is to convince myself that it's okay to sing again…I very much appreciate and thank every 'woman with wings' for coming into my life." **Meg P., Woodbury, MN**

It's Thursday Night! Singing in Sacred Circle

Women With Wings has been meeting at the Unitarian Universalist Church at 120 Park Street in Bangor, Maine since October 1993. We meet from 7:00-9:00 pm in a large room called the vestry. It helps that we meet at the same time in the same place every week so that regulars and visitors can be certain of finding the comfort and the stimulation of the singing circle without fuss or bother. The UU Church has been most generous in letting us use the space and we, in turn, give a weekly donation and take very good care of the gift we are given.

The first years were a bit challenging as we struggled to find a format that worked for the good of the group. We dealt with power struggles, different ways of making decisions, opposing theologies and questions about our purpose and mission. Happily, we have developed a pattern for our Thursday evenings that is simple and works very well. The routine provides a very loose structure that is freeing because everyone knows what is going to happen next and the circle happens whether there are four or forty women present to sing. We present the following outline for you to share with your group. Use what works for you and make the changes necessary to be comfortable, safe and inspired.

Women arriving before 7:00 pm arrange the chairs in a circle and decorate the altar- a simple table placed in the middle of the circle.

7:00 pm - Gathering – All present form a circle around the altar, standing in front of the chairs. One woman starts a chant or song and it is sung until it feels finished (at least three times) and then another one is started. One chant seems to suggest the next one and the women take turns starting or suggesting which song should be next. The circle expands as women continue to arrive and enter.

7:30 pm - Names - Everyone sits and a leader (anyone who wants to!) explains that we will now go around the circle and each woman will say, sing, and/or act out the name she wants to be known by for the evening. Each woman has a turn and the group responds by echoing her name/action in as identical a manner as possible. After each woman has been heard and recognized, the group stands and sings, "We enter this circle in trust and faith." We then ask for anyone having a birthday that week to go into the center of the circle and we sing our happy birthday song while those with a birthday go around to each woman in the circle, do a general wave, or their very own birthday dance. The birthday women are then asked how old they are and the oldest receives her "birthday treatment" while the others return to the circle until their turn comes. The woman standing in the circle is gifted with our birthday chant and a toning using her name. She then is asked what song/chant she would like the group to sing to her. When her song is finished, the next woman enters the center and the sequence is repeated. After that we put names into the circle for healing and return to singing whatever chants are begun.

8:00 pm – Break – we turn on the lights and sit in our chairs while a basket is passed for a $3.00 donation to pay our rent and our director. Announcements are given by any woman who has one and then we sing a closing song to acknowledge that some may not return after the break. We take ten minutes to visit, get water or use the restroom and then we come back into the circle.

8:15 – 9:00 pm – Singing – The last forty-five minutes are when new songs or chants are taught or we return to the free form of singing and dancing. We always end on time, closing with "Merry Meet and Merry Part and Merry Meet Again."

We believe that flexibility has been an important element in our success. Women come and go as they are able. Attendance is not required. Everything is done on a volunteer basis with the exception of our director who receives a small stipend.

Because we learn our chants and songs by listening, there is rarely any paper in the circle and women are looking at each other rather than at the music. It seems that once a chant or song has been committed to memory, it is always available and we now have hundreds of chants and songs to instantly draw upon. All it takes is for one of us to start the first line and soon everyone is singing with her.

Although we may not totally understand it, we know that our singing circle is changing our lives. We may not see it in ourselves but we see it in each other. As we find our voices, we are finding ourselves and each other as beautiful women with limitless possibilities. We have indeed become Women With Wings. **Colleen Fitzgerald**

Jami Cass

Wings Sings On

When Kay Gardner died on August 28, 2002, she left behind our tightly woven circle of women who sing and celebrate together every week. Kay was the founding music director of Women With Wings and was instrumental in the weaving of this circle. For many of us, she was the midwife to the birth of our musically creative selves. None of us had written songs before joining this group but Kay opened us up to that possibility. Now we have this songbook with seventy nine songs created by the women who sing on Thursday nights.

Kay also left this circle deeply shaken at the sudden and unexpected loss of our beloved, vibrant and amazing friend. On the Thursday after her death, Women With Wings met and we cried, wailed, sang, and hugged. We held each other up through that most painful time. We sang at her memorial service, which ended with joyful drumming, dancing and singing.

Going through a traumatic experience can either pull people apart or draw them more closely together. Wings had two performances scheduled for early September and we decided to honor those commitments. One of our members says she believes that having to pull ourselves together for these events helped keep us from falling apart as a group. We found ourselves deeply bound to each other in loving, caring relationship.

Our singing has evolved out of this experience and this bond. We now sing deeply from our hearts and our power. It truly feels like music as medicine. We do not sing to entertain. We sing to create sacred space, in which people can heal, unlock emotions that have kept them stuck, and celebrate all aspects of life. Our singing has become a vehicle for opening ourselves to our essence and connecting with the essence of others.

We do perform several times a year, usually to benefit organizations that support women or environmental causes. We have a CD with original chants and within the next few years, we will have another. The magic of what we do is not really in listening to us sing. The magic is in the singing. So grab some friends (or strangers), learn some chants, and sing! Let the music flow through you; let it open you. Create your own sacred singing circle. If you find yourself in Bangor, Maine on a Thursday evening at 7:00 pm, drop into the Unitarian Universalist Society of Bangor and join us for an evening of soul-massaging singing. We plan to be there forever.

> In harmony,
> Linda Smith Koehler
> Music Director of Women with Wings

Acknowledgements

It has been said that there are only two prayers: "Help me, Help me, Help me." and "Thank you, Thank you, Thank you." The first prayer was used a lot in the making of this songbook, especially after Kay hung up her earthly cloak and passed to other planes of existence. It is now time for the second prayer.

So very many women helped to make this book in your hands a reality, it will be difficult to acknowledge all of them. First and foremost, it is necessary to repeat that Kay Gardner was our inspiration. Her vision of a CD of our songs that could go out into the world to touch the lives of women in need of this special brand of healing became a reality in the summer of 2002. The CD "Hand in Hand & Heart to Heart" that Kay produced was finished in time for her to take it to the last Michigan Women's Music Festival she would attend. We had begun the process of creating a songbook to go along with it and before she left for Michigan, Kay gave me her introduction and the blurbs for her own songs which are included. Did she intuitively know she wouldn't have time to do it later? We are grateful for her guidance and the words she chose to introduce this book.

Many women helped in various ways to create this songbook. A committee was formed to tackle the job. Committee members and Wingers who worked on this project are: Colleen Fitzgerald, Grace Walker, Jami Cass, Jeanne Bradley, Linda Koehler, Lise Herold, Louise Shorette, Maryann Ingalls, Mida Ballard, Pam Healy, Rose Iuro-Damon, Sandy Imondi, and probably others I have missed mentioning. It should be said, at this point, that without Deb Burwell's recommendation that Wings adopt the guidelines from Peace and Power: Building Communities for the Future by Peggy L. Chin for any decision making, the time spent in committee would have been much more difficult.

Linda Koehler is our current director and the task of completing the music portion of the songbook fell heavily on her shoulders. Kay had completed the music notation for all the songs on the CD, her own songs and a few others. With seventy-nine songs going into the book, more than half the songs had not been notated. We are very grateful to Linda - gifted singer, songwriter, director, wife, mother of two boys and teacher – for the time and energy it took to complete the music notation that no other Winger was capable of doing. A special thanks to the goddess of snow days for providing Linda with the time to complete the task this past winter.

This book holds the creative gifts from Wingers that come in the form of songs, writings, poems, artwork and the loving healing energy included for all to partake of. One of our members, Robin Fre, was especially helpful with her talent for writing and knowledge of spiritual matters. Before she moved to upstate New York she offered to help by writing anything we might need for the book. I asked her to come up with an explanatory paragraph for each of the six categories we chose for the songs. She gave us license to use any or all of what she had written for us about these categories and her words became the seeds for what you now read at the beginning of each section in the songbook.

Additional thanks go to Colleen Fitzgerald, Kay's partner, for providing the dedication for the book. As one Winger put it, "She said exactly what I would have said if I were able to write anything coherent at all."

So here you have it, our first songbook is in your hands directly from our hearts. We trust that you will gain as much in the receiving as we have in the giving. We also trust that you will now join us in giving loving, vibrational healing and empowerment to others.

Thank you, thank you, thank you,
Mida Ballard
Songbook Coordinator

Songs
Of
Affirmation

Affirmation: to make a positive statement with conviction.
Our voices declare our intent and affirm ourselves as divinely feminine and creative. As we sing aloud, we create our own realities, choosing who we are and whom we present to the world. With rhythm and song, we voice our declarations with intent.

3

Women With Wings
Purpose

Linda J Smith Koehler
Copyright 1998

As var - ied strands we gath - er, To weave our sac - red
pow - er of each voice, - - A great - er voice is
sing to hon - or Moth - er Earth, We cher - ish wo - man -

ring. We join our hands in cir - cle, And from our hearts we
born, We send our heal - ing sound to soothe, The souls that have been
hood, In songs from all a - round the world, We join for great - er

chorus

sing. Our sing - ing brings us pow - er. Our sing - ing sets us
torn.
good.

free. The har - mo - ny of song to - geth - er, brings great joy to

1   2   3

me.

From the me.

We me.

"Our Statement of Purpose was written by three of our founding members, Pam Gross, Colleen Fitzgerald, and Kay Gardner in 1993. I used their words and ideas to write the poem for this song in 1996."

Celebrate

Ina
copyright 2002

Cel - e - brate, cel - e - brate, Cel - e - brate, cel - e -

brate, Cel - e - brate, cel - e - brate life. We

are at one with the un - i - verse, We

are at one with the un - i - verse.

Dance and sing and let your heart song ring.

Dance and sing and let your heart song ring.

Cel - e - brate, cel - e - brate, Cel - e - brate, cel - e - brate,

Cel - e - brate, cel - e - brate life.

I Am

Linda J Smith Koehler
Copyright 1999

Hold the "Am" note on "mmm" rather than the "a."

example of how next repeat would be

✻ Repeat ad. infin. Each time the song is repeated, start in the key last sung. It will climb higher each time it is repeated.

"I believe we are complex beings and that we have the power, at least to some extent, to create who we are. This song is an affirmation of who I wish we could all be."

A Place

Liddy Lindsay
copyright 2001

Thrive

Ina
copyright 2002

Shake your bo-dy move it all a-round. Sink your roots in-

to the ground. Sway your branch-es like a tree. Don't

for-get to breathe and just be. Be like a bird who flies

through the air or hunk-er down and walk like a bear.

You can blos-som and smell like a rose or be-come the o-cean that

ebbs and flows. You can jump in-to the wat-er and swim like a fish.

You can be an-y-thing that you wish. So breathe and move and let

your-self thrive and give great thanks for be-ing a-live and

give great thanks for be-ing a-live.

Ancestors

Ina
copyright 2002

"This came to me while I was in a ceremonial space. I went to my ancestors to ask for help with a ritual I was preparing."

Responsibility

Ina
copyright 2002

Take re-spon-si-bi-li-ty for your-self! With ev'-ry thought and word and deed, you

can de-cide where there's a need to change, yes change!

Change the way you think a-bout your-self, change what words come out of your mouth,

change how you move and act in the world and you will see a new life un-furl,

one that is wise and lov - ing and kind, one that frees you heart, your soul and your mind.

When we take re-spon - si-bi - li-ty we cre - ate a bet-ter world for you and me. So

won't cha come and join me please and be will-ing to take re-spon-si-bi-li-ty?

Won't cha come and join me please and be will-ing to take re-spon-si-bi-li-ty?

Dancing With The Darkness

Ina
copyright 2002

Emergence

Rose Iuro-Damon
copyright 2002

Everything Beautiful

Colleen Fitzgerald
copyright 2002

1.Ev - 'ry - thing beau - ti - ful in me is ris - ing,

Ev - 'ry - thing beau - ti - ful bloom - ing in me,

Spir - it - ual beau - ty is ris - ing to sur - face,

Fine

My sis - ters' eyes hold the mir - ror for me.

2.Sing of the sea - sons that cir - cle a - round us,
3.When we're to - geth - er we gath - er in cir - cles,

Sing of the joy that each mo - ment can bring,
Join - ing our voi - ces we raise en - er - gy,

Sing of the col - ors and heal - ing vi - bra - tions,
Each strong a - lone and strong - er to - geth - er,

D.C. al Fine

Play - ing a love song on Na - ture's heart - strings.
Cir - cles and spi - rals new pat - terns we see.

Holy Ground

15

Linda J Smith Koehler
copyright 2001

"I have a beautiful drive to work, right beside the Penobscot River heading north from Orono. In the warmer months, I frequently see great blue herons and bald eagles fishing. In the winter, I love to watch the river seize up into ice then ease back down into its fluid self in the spring. On a very clear day, I get a brief view of Mt. Katahdin, the highest peak in Maine. This daily drive through the wonder of Nature has inspired a number of my songs. (Yes, I write a lot of my songs in the car!)

"I fervently believe that we humans are capable of living in a peaceful and respectful way together. I also believe that each of us is a piece of the whole that is our source. My reverence for Nature and for the divinity within each and every human being brought me to this song."

Hand In Hand And Heart To Heart

(River Of Love)

Dona Stover
copyright 2002

Hand in hand and heart to heart, Ov - er the hills and through the dark, You light my way, I can see your spark, Home to the riv - er of love. Home to the shores of pine and rock, Home to the riv - er of the eag - le and hawk, My heart yearns to love this spot, Home to the riv - er of love.

"Written on a return trip from Bangor to Calais following a regular Thursday night circle sing at Wings. I was singing this song to myself when I had a head on collision with a bull moose on Route 9. The moose died, my van was wrecked, but I was unscathed. I felt a veil of protection descend between me and the moose upon impact."

I Create Peace

Linda J Smith Koehler
Copyright 2001

I can-not change the world, I can on - ly change my-self.

When I make change in my-self, I cre-ate change in the

world. I be - come like the stone, and when I am thrown, in - to the

sea of peo - ple, Those chang - es in me rip-ple out

through that sea, in ev - er wid - en-ing cir - cles, So I cre-ate Peace,

I send you Love. I cre-ate Peace, I send you Love.

Chant to be sung many times

"This was my second post-September 11th song. The chant at the end came first then the prologue. The chant is meant to be sung freely, with people harmonizing and starting at various points to give it the ripping round effect. Experiment with it until you find a way that sounds good to you."

Below, The Earth Reveals My Path

Linda J Smith Koehler
Copyright 2001

And so be-low the earth re-veals my path,

And so a-bove the stars guide my way,

And so with-in I find the strength to live,

And keep on liv-ing day af-ter day.

"This song was created during a walk through the woods near my house. I frequently get lost back there because the trails twist and turn unpredictably. I seldom end off where I intended but I am always grateful for the journey the trails lead me on."

River Of Love

Sofia Patience Wilder
copyright 2002

My riv - er of love flows to the sea, Where the Great Moth - er

I repeat several times

waits to send love to me. My

2

me So __ Fly down the riv - er to me, Fly down the riv - er ea - gle,

Fly down the riv - er to me show me the way. My prayer soars high on your

wings in the Moth - er Sky. Fly down the riv - er to me, Fly down the riv - er ea - gle,

Fly down the riv - er to me, show me the way.

"I sit on the porch of my home every day of the year and watch the Penobscot River roll by. Eagles (sometimes five and six at a time) will fly down this majestic, magical body of water. This song came to me one day when the eagle flew."

Knowing Love

Sofia Patience Wilder
copyright 2002

Know - ing love, my heart is o - pen to the sky. Know - ing

love, my heart is o - pen to the sky. Know - ing love, my heart is

o - pen to the sky. Know - ing love, my heart is o - pen.

" 'Knowing love, my heart is open to the sky' is a line from the Kama Sutra. One beautiful summer day I floated in the Stillwater River, feeling immersed in love and this song came to me."

Kitchen Boogie

Sofia Patience Wilder
copyright 2002

"I love to wash dishes – hot water and bubbles and singing – what could be better? This song came as I washed dishes; but I've struggled with the lyrics over the years. I feel this song has evolved into a more powerful place, from 'Clap your hands, stamp your feet' to 'Clap your hands, catch the heat.'"

Mama Don't Want

Lynn Flewelling
copyright 2002

♩ = 120

1. Ma-ma dont want no Bar-bie Doll waist-line. Ma-ma dont want no
2. Ma-ma got hips to car-ry the ba-bies. Ma-ma got breasts to
3. Ma-ma dont need no spec-ial treat-ment. Ma-ma dont want no

plat-in-num hair. Ma-ma dont want no minks and dia-monds.
feed 'em right. Ma-ma dont need no pent-house hust-ler,
La-dies' Night. Ma-ma dont need no dis-pen-sa-tion. It's

Just wants the re-spect that's fair.
tellin' her what she's all a-bout.
e-qual pay gon-na set things right.

"I'd been listening to a lot of Etta James and Uppity Blues Women. This one just slipped out. Sing it honky tonk from the belly with lots of sass and bounce."

No More Masks

Maryann Ingalls
copyright 2002

No more masks. No more masks. No more masks. No more masks. I am the one you see be - fore you, and you are the one who stands be - fore me. No more No more masks. No more masks. No more masks.

"Women With Wings has taught me a great deal about the gifts we can be to one another, if we are only willing to be ourselves and let others be themselves."

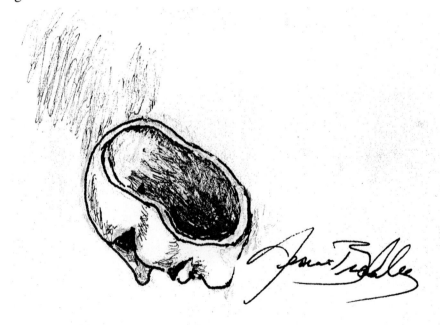

Beachcomber

Maryann Ingalls
copyright 2002

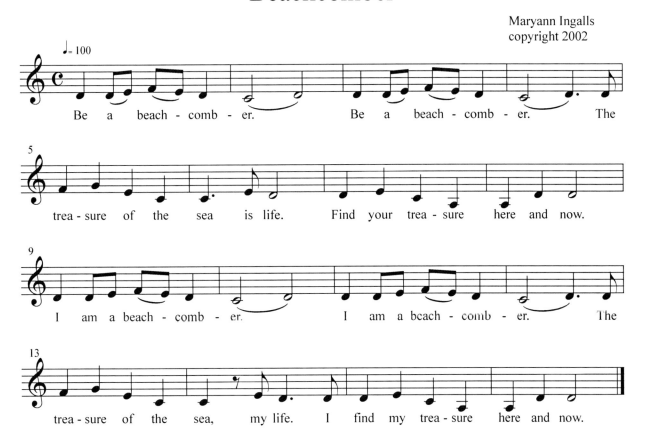

♩ = 100

Be a beach - comb - er. Be a beach - comb - er. The

5 trea - sure of the sea is life. Find your trea - sure here and now.

9 I am a beach - comb - er. I am a beach - comb - er. The

13 trea - sure of the sea, my life. I find my trea - sure here and now.

"I love to comb the beach. It is a very mindful, relaxing practice. And, it reminds me to be mindful of the rest of my life, to not miss any of its wonderful gifts. This is the first song I ever wrote."

Be Here Now

Debbie J. Christo
copyright 2002

♩=100

Now is the on - ly mo - ment. Now is the on - ly

mo - ment. Be in this mo - ment. Breathe in this mo - ment.

Love in this mo - ment. Be here now.

Be here now in this mo - ment.

Now is the on - ly mo - ment. Now is the on - ly mo - ment.

Be in this mo - ment. Breathe in this mo - ment. Love in this mo - ment.

Be here now. Be here now in this mo - ment.

"Thich Nhat Hanh is a Vietnamese Zen master, poet and peace advocate who currently resides in a small village in Southern France. In July 1994, I had the privilege of attending a 'mindful living' retreat there, under his direction. This song, was born of that experience and I often think of it as my 'mantra' – a gift from the spirit that serves to remind me to live fully in the present moment. May it serve you well."

Everything That Ever Was

Debbie Christo
copyright 2002

Ev' - ry - thing that ev - er was will be. Ev' - ry - thing that will be

has al - ways been. Chang - ing, chang - ing, yet

ev - er the same. Chang - ing, chang - ing, come 'round a - gain.

"This song sprang from that sudden 'knowing' that everything (on a molecular level) that has ever existed, still exists, that life and death are only change. We are truly a part of everything and everything is a part of us. How might our world be if we all lived with this awareness?"

Trust

Ina
copyright 2002

I can see the light that shines with-in you. I can feel the beat of your heart.

I can see the light that shines with-in you. I can feel the beat of your heart.

Trust in the light of love, the pulse of the un - i - verse.

Trust in the light of love, the pow - er of the un - i - verse.

"These songs reflect the times in my life when I was so full of what was happening that there was no more room for it inside and it spilled out, scribbled onto scraps of paper or sung into my voice mail with the greatest sense of wonder and gratitude. That's the way it happens, I don't sit down to write them, they just blow in no matter where I am. When I'm having one of those overly full moments I gotta write them down quick or sing them into my voice mail. "

Hold Up Your Head

Lynn Flewelling
copyright 2002

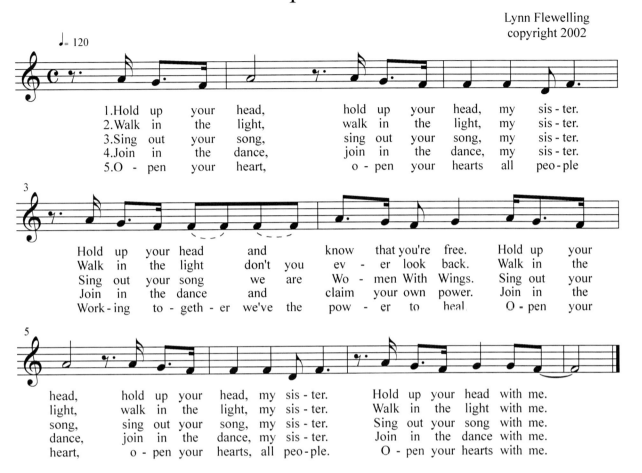

1. Hold up your head, hold up your head, my sis-ter.
2. Walk in the light, walk in the light, my sis-ter.
3. Sing out your song, sing out your song, my sis-ter.
4. Join in the dance, join in the dance, my sis-ter.
5. O-pen your heart, o-pen your hearts all peo-ple

Hold up your head and know that you're free. Hold up your
Walk in the light don't you ev - er look back. Walk in the
Sing out your song we are Wo - men With Wings. Sing out your
Join in the dance and claim your own power. Join in the
Work-ing to-geth-er we've the pow - er to heal. O-pen your

head, hold up your head, my sis-ter. Hold up your head with me.
light, walk in the light, my sis-ter. Walk in the light with me.
song, sing out your song, my sis-ter. Sing out your song with me.
dance, join in the dance, my sis-ter. Join in the dance with me.
heart, o - pen your hearts, all peo-ple. O - pen your hearts with me.

"Kay and Women With Wings introduced me to a type of music I'd never heard before, and a new type of performance. In the early days there was no sheet music, no rehearsal. We just taught each other what we knew by ear, and everyone wove in their own sound. It was beautiful and very freeing. Most of those songs were on the somber side, though – mystical, thoughtful, even sad, and often in a minor key. I wanted to hear all those lovely voices singing something lively, a song to summon up the deep down power and dignity we all possess, so I wrote this. Clap your hands when you sing this one, sisters, move those hips, and don't ever sing it slow!"

Anything Is Possible

Jami Cass
copyright 2002

An - y - thing is pos - si - ble. An - y - thing is pos - si - ble.

An - y - thing is pos - si - ble. An - y - thing is ble.

"This song came to me from a common response that I hear myself saying to my three children… an idealist at heart, I like to think that anything is possible. When I sing it to them, or they sing it to me, it sounds different than when we sing it in circle: the last notes are strange and only Kay seemed to always sing them most beautifully."

Beauty

Grace Walker
copyright 2002

Beau - ty is all a - round us, Our thoughts bring it in - to be - ing,

Peace is all a - round us, Our jour - ney makes it so.

"The inspiration for this song came after reading Voices of Our Ancestors – Cherokee Teachings From the Wisdom Fire by Dhyani Ywahoo. She is the founder and director of Sunray Meditation Society, an international spiritual society dedicated to planetary peace."

Listen

Pam Healy
copyright 2002

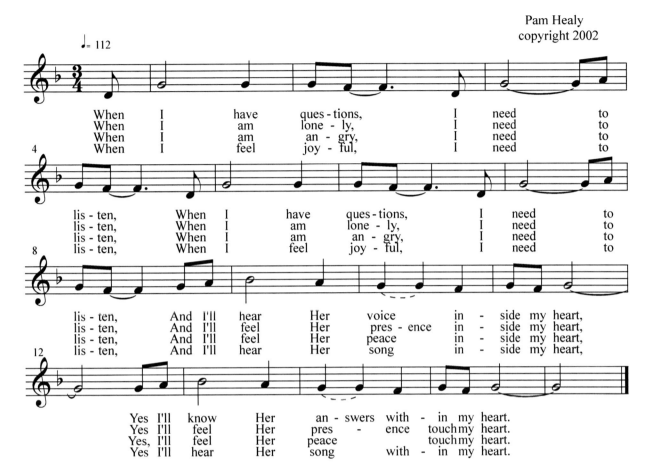

"A lot of inspiration for the songs comes from the ocean during a walk on the beach.
The Goddess has given me a great gift – the song comes from Her."

I Go Up To The Mountain

Linda J Smith Koehler
Copyright 2002

I go up to the moun-tain to find my an-swers, I go
down to the o-cean to find my peace, I go in-to the for-est to
find con-nec-tion, I lie down in the sun-ny grass to feel at home.

"This song is a reflection of how I commune with the divine. I wrote it while driving south beside the Penobscot River toward Alamoosook Lake. While there, my parents, my two sons and I walked across its frozen surface to the islands in the middle. These kinds of outings were my church as a child. On Sundays when my friends were in buildings worshipping, my family was at some beautiful spot in the glory of Nature. We would hike, swim, or sled and, in my mind, worship the wonders around us."

Let My Drum Beat

Rose Iuro-Damon
copyright 2002

Let my drum beat to my heart, My bo-dy dance to my soul, Let my voice sail in the wind, My spir-it cir-cle whole.

"During a UU women's retreat a Hersey, I thought about what being there truly meant to me. Here it is!"

I Am A Beautiful Woman

Hila Shooter
age 7

Hila's mother, Flic, writes – As we were driving home from Wings the other night my daughter, Hila, was glowing with pride and delight that people like her song and wanted to sing it. She went on to say, "But Mum, it's not really mine, I just started singing it. I heard it in my head, bits at first, and then all of it. And then it was a real song."

I went on to explain that when we get inspiration like that I think it's a gift from the universe. "But why did it come to me?" she wanted to know. "Perhaps because you were the best person for the job." "Yes, but I'm just a kid." "True, but when you get a gift from the universe, I think that it is for passing on; giving away to make the world a better place, and that's what you did." "But how could my song do that?" "Well, imagine a woman living with a partner who was really mean to her, who told her every day she was ugly, clumsy and not good at anything. What would be the smart thing for a woman to do in that situation?" "Leave of course." "But sometimes that is hard. The woman might believe the things that her partner was telling her and feel really bad about herself. Then she might hear your song, and gradually, as she sings it over and over in her head and then on her lips, she begins to believe that perhaps your song tells the truth and gradually she summons the courage to leave."

"So that is why it came to me? So I could pass it on?"

Everything Will Be All Right

Kay Gardner
copyright 2002

Ev - 'ry - thing will be all right,

Day is day and fol - lows night,

Ev - 'ry - thing will be all right,

Dark - ness flows in - to the light.

"You can never tell when a chant will come to inspire or heal you. This affirmation came to me while in the car. My transmission broke down, and I sang this chant for the twenty-or-so miles I needed to travel to my mechanic's garage."

See illustration on next page:

Women With Wings has been a safe space for me to heal, and grow with the encouragement and friendship of a circle of women and Kay Gardner. Kay encouraged me to listen, to feel the healing power of sound and to eventually find my own voice.

In discovering my own voice "Bones and Stone" was born. It initially began as a piece of artwork for this songbook, but as the drawing neared it's completion it took on a life of its own. The calligraphy flowed without thought. I felt the words were a gift from the "Mother!" The following day, while traveling in my car, the melody came to me and the song "Bones and Stone" was born.

This is a song of celebration, an affirmation honoring life's passages and the ever-turning spiral, "forever turning home." On the day Kay Gardner was cremated "Bones and Stone" was one of the many songs sung in circle by women gathered in front of the crematorium who stood vigil and honored her passing and again at the Summer Solstice memorial for Kay held on Stonington, Deer Isle.

"Bones and Stone" is dedicated to Kay Gardner who encouraged, inspired and guided me on the spiritual path of song and finding my own voice. Gentle Blessing In Her Name!

Louise Shorette

Mother Earth Songs

We embrace Earth as our mother. Through these songs we honor and celebrate her abundance; our food, the air we breathe, the waters, and the very ground beneath our feet. Drawing on the energy of Mother Earth we sing to restore balance and harmony to the world.

Forgive Us, Mother Earth

Colleen Fitzgerald
copyright 2002

♩= 88

For - give us Moth - er Earth, for we know not what we do. For -
give us Fath - er Sky, for the dam - age done to you. We knew the truth so
ver - y long a - go, The web of life con - nects us all. We are not here a - lone. We

verses

are not here a - lone. 1.The en - er - gy in you is the en - er - gy in me, The
en - er - gy's the same in ev' - ry flow - er, rock and tree. The an - i - mals and birds share our
com - mon space, There's more to life on Earth than just a hu - man face. For -

2.When we simplify our lives, we can see what really counts.
 It's the quality of life not status or amount.
With an attitude of gratitude, humility and awe,
We learn that loving compassion is the universal law.

3.The Twenty-First Century has come into our view,
 Giving us a vision of a world begun anew.
 We can stand together, join our voices and our hearts,
 With women, men, and children, no longer torn apart.

"This song came to me while showering. I must have been thinking about the coming of the new millennium and the progress that has or has not been made by the inhabitants of our planet. I believe we have lost a sense of what is most important: we are not here alone and what we do has great impact on everything and everyone around us for many generations."

Earth's Lullaby

Linda J Smith Koehler
Copyright 1998

Great   Moth-er   Earth,   crad - le   me   in your   lov - ing arms,
Great   Moth-er   Earth,   crad - le   me   in your   lov - ing arms,

Sing   me   your   o - cean - pound - ing   lul - la - by,   lul - la - by,   Car -
Sing   me   your   o - cean - pound - ing   lul - la - by,   lul - la - by,   Car -

ess   my   face   with your   warm   soft   breez - es,
ess   my   face   with your   warm   soft   breez - es,

Let   Grand - ma   Moon   shine   through your   clear   skies.
Let   Fath - er   Sun   shine   through your   clear   skies.

Rock Me, Mama

Linda J Smith Koehler
Copyright 1999

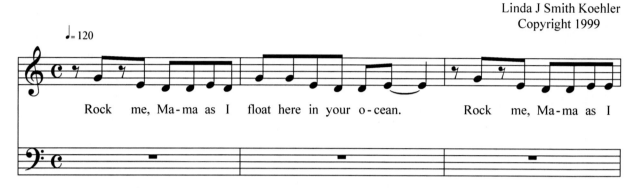

Rock me, Ma-ma as I float here in your o-cean. Rock me, Ma-ma as I

float here in your sea. Rock me, Ma-ma as I clar-if-y e-mo-tion.

Rock me, Ma-ma, make me true to me.

Rock me, Ma-ma, Ma-ma,

Rock me, Ma-ma, Rock me, Ma-ma, make me true to me.

"The waves rocked me gently and I felt like pure potential in the Earth's womb."

All That Is

Ina
copyright 2002

"This song came to me one Christmas day while sitting alone in the woods by a fairy castle."

Gratitude

Ina
copyright 2002

♩=120

I thank the earth for feed-ing my bod - y. I thank the sun for

warm-in' my bones. I thank the trees for the air I breathe, an'

I thank the wat - er for nour - ish - ing my soul.

harmony

I thank the earth for feed-ing my bod - y. I thank the sun for

warm-in' my bones. I thank the trees for the air I breathe, an'

I thank the wat - er for nour - ish - ing my soul.

"This song came to me while driving down to Virginia. As the sun was going down, four spec-tacular hot air balloons rose over the horizon. It was an absolutely glorious sight and this song came to me."

Garden Round

Kay Gardner
copyright 2002

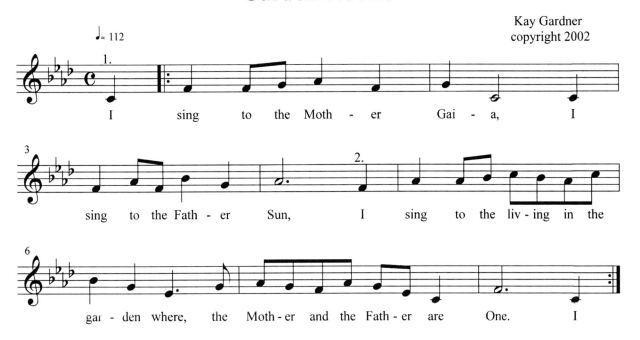

I sing to the Moth - er Gai - a, I sing to the Fath - er Sun, I sing to the liv - ing in the gar - den where, the Moth - er and the Fath - er are One. I

Seed By Seed

Jami Cass
copyright 2002

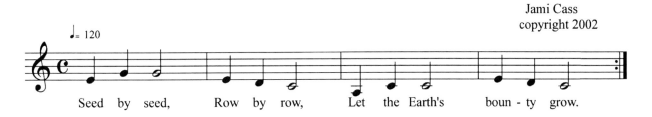

Seed by seed, Row by row, Let the Earth's boun - ty grow.

Plant Your Feet

Linda J Smith Koehler
Copyright 1999

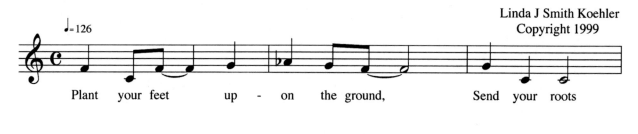

Plant your feet up - on the ground, Send your roots

spi - ral - ling down, Feel the en - er - gy of the Earth,

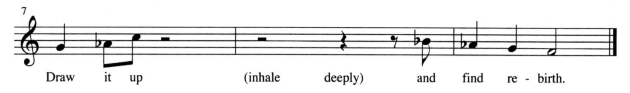

Draw it up (inhale deeply) and find re - birth.

"I went to a weekend retreat with Starhawk. At lunch some of the participants were discussing the importance of grounding during or at the end of ritual. This song was a response to that need."

Cycles Of Life

A Round

Janet Ciano
copyright 2002

Cy - cles of life, Sea - sons of the year,

Rhy - thms of the Earth, In my heart beat.

Sister Crow

Dona Stover
copyright 2002

Sis-ter Crow, Sis-ter Crow, Fly-ing through the sky, Sis-ter Crow, Sis-ter Crow,

take me wing on high, Sis-ter Crow, Sis-ter Crow, do your dance with me,

wrap me in your feath-ers of the black-est eb-on-y.

"Written on a trip to Bangor from Calais to attend a regular Thursday night circle sing at Wings. That evening crows kept rising up into the sky again and again as I made my way along Route 9."

Goddess Songs

we are the ones
We've been
Waiting
for.....

©Louise M. Shorette

By singing songs that recognize the feminine divine, we honor the Goddess in each of us. We honor ourselves. With songs that speak to and strengthen all aspects of women, we are indeed empowered.

I Am Your Legacy

Echo C. Aven
copyright 2002

Moth - er of Mys - ter - y, I am your leg - a - cy.

Teach me to weave so fine, as I dance and I spin through time.

Shim - mer - ing end - less - ly, wov - en in mys - ter - y, in ev - er - y thing I see, your

web of pure en - er - gy. Moth - er of Mys - ter - y, I am your

leg - a - cy. From each finger a gold - en strand, join - ing each hand to each

hand. Shim - mer - ing end - less - ly, wov - en in mys - ter - y, in ev - er - y - thing I see, your

web of pure en - er - gy. Moth - er of Mys - ter - y,

I am your leg - a - cy. I am your leg - a - cy.

Invocation

Ina
copyright 2002

Earth Moth-er, Earth Moth-er, I'm call-in' out to you.

Won't you come and be with me and teach me of your truth.

Teach me a-bout nur-tur-ing, Teach me to be strong,

Teach me how to give and re-ceive all the day long.

2) Hecate, Hecate, I'm callin' out to you.
Won't you come and be with me
and teach me of your truth?
Teach me about light and dark and of the place within.
Teach me about life and death and how to shed my skin.

3) Quan Yin, Quan Yin, I'm callin' out to you.
Won't you come and be with me
and teach me of your truth?
Teach me about gentleness, teach me to be kind.
Teach me about peace and love, it's what I seek to find.

4) Kali-ma, Kali-ma, I'm callin' out to you.
Won't you come and be with me
and teach me of your truth?
Teach me about fire and how it can destroy.
Teach me how to take this light and turn it into joy.

5) Cybelle, Cybelle, I'm callin' out to you.
Won't you come and be with me
and teach me of your truth?
Teach me to be joyous, to dance and drum and sing.
Teach me how to open wide and let my heart song ring.

6) Aphrodite, Aphrodite, I'm callin' out to you.
Won't you come and be with me
and teach me of your truth?
Teach me about pleasure, teach me about love.
Teach me sensuality, it's what I've been dreaming of.

7) Isis, Mighty Isis, I'm callin' out to you.
Won't you come and be with me
and teach me of your truth?
Teach me about power, the source that's deep inside.
Teach me how to see the light that in all things resides.

* Each verse is varies slightly.

Oh Mighty Isis

Linda J Smith Koehler
Copyright 1998

air journeys: Oh Might - y Is - is, spread your wings be-neath us and
land journeys: Oh Might - y Is - is, spread your wings be-neath us and
or: Oh Moth - er Is - is

lift us safe - ly to the sky. Oh Might - y Is - is,
guide us safe - ly on our way. Oh Might - y Is - is,

wrap your wings a-round us and take us safe - ly home a - gain.
wrap your wings a-round us and take us safe - ly home a - gain.

"This song came to me while sitting on the runway in a jet plane several hours after experiencing an emergency landing in a small propeller plane. We were greeted by fire trucks and people in silver asbestos suits. Everyone was physically fine but our nerves were shot. I needed something to help me remain calm while I sat on the runway waiting for the next take-off. A friend had told me how she imagined the Egyptian goddess, Isis, flying with her golden wings spread beneath the plane. This image comforted me and this song came from that. I sang it for the first ten minutes of the flight and again at landing. Now at Wings whenever anyone is traveling, we sing this for them. For travel by land we sing, '…and guide us safely on our way…' instead of '…lift us safely to the sky…'."

The Goddess Is In Me

Deb Chapman
copyright 2002

Crescent Moon
Over the mountains
Crimson into indigo,
For this moment I was born.

By Louise Shorette (September 1999)

Moon Songs

Ina

Through the ages, the moon has often been referred to as female. When we honor the moon, we honor cycles we share. The moon waxes and wanes, controlling the oceans' tides, controlling moods and sentiments. The moon is a symbol of ancient wisdom, of creative spirituality, and of womanhood. When we sing songs honoring the moon, we honor ourselves.

Fabulous Moon

Rose Iuro-Damon
copyright 2002

Oh Oh Oh you fab-u-lous moon, You send your sil-ver mag-ic and make me bloom. In lun-a dance I'm wild, For-ev-er I'm your child, Up-on my life you've smiled, Down on me, Set-tin' me free, Fab-u-lous moon,

repeat several times

ending *rit.*

Fab-u-lous moon. Gon-na get me some of that Fab-u-lous moon.

"Gazing with admiration at a particularly fabulous full moon, this song burst forth!"

The Man in the Moon is a lady
A lady of satin and pearls
The cow that jumped over
Said, "Jumping Jehovah!
I knew it! She's one of the girls!"

Dancing Mother Moon

Rose Iuro-Damon
copyright 2002

Danc - ing   Moth - er   Moon,   Light   my   nights and   noons.

Keep me glow-ing,   keep me grow-ing,   fad-ing   full and   new.

Bask - ing   in your   gleam,   Il - lum - in-mate   my   dreams.

Keep me chang-ing,   re - ar - rang-ing,   Maid-en   Moth-er   Crone.

"Walking on a sweet summer evening over a footbridge on my favorite cove,
I watched the moon dance in the water and this song came to me."

She plays with the stars and the planets
She throws the Big Dipper a kiss
So don't you offend her
Remember her gender
The Man in the Moon is a Ms.!

Source Unknown

Goddess Of The Moon

Linda J Smith Koehler
Copyright 1996

God - dess of the moon _ you shine bright - ly through day and night.
God - dess of the moon _ you shine bright - ly through day and night.
God - dess of the moon _ you shine bright - ly through day and night.

God - dess of the moon _ you il - lu - min - ate the phas - es of my life.
God - dess of the moon _ you il - lu - min - ate the phas - es of my life.
God - dess of the moon _ you il - lu - min - ate the phas - es of my life.

New_ moon, new_ ba - by, in - no - cent and o - pen.
Blos - soming moon, blos-soming maid - en, grow-ing in - to wo - man.
Wan - ing moon wis - en-ing wo - man, spir - it ev - er strong - er.

Smil-ing cres - ent, smil-ing child, danc-ing through the flow - ers.
Full moon, full moth - er birth - ing a new life.
Fad - ing cres - ent, fad-ing crone, pass-ing to a new plane.

"I was enchanted by the cycles of the moon and the idea that its phases reflect the cycle of women's lives. This idea percolated in my mind for quite a while. One night while driving home from Wings, under a waning gibbous moon, this song came to me."

Grandmother Moon

Ina
copyright 2002

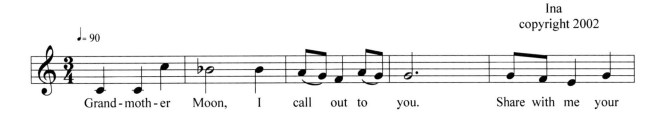

Grand-moth-er Moon, I call out to you. Share with me your

pow - er when you're full and you're new. Grand-moth - er Moon,

shine down on me. Share with me your pow-er. Set my soul free.

"These songs reflect the times in my life when I was so full of what was happening that there was no more room for it inside and it spilled out, scribbled onto scraps of paper or sung into my voice mail with the greatest sense of wonder and gratitude. That's the way it happens, I don't sit down to write them, they just blow in no matter where I am. When I'm having one of those overly full moments I gotta write them down quick or sing them into my voice mail."

Healing
Songs

The vibrational energy of sound in singing healing songs brings us into balance. In gathering and in channeling energy through song, we create healing power. As we sing, we send loving energy that ripples outward with healing intent.

One Of These Days

Colleen Fitzgerald
copyright 2002

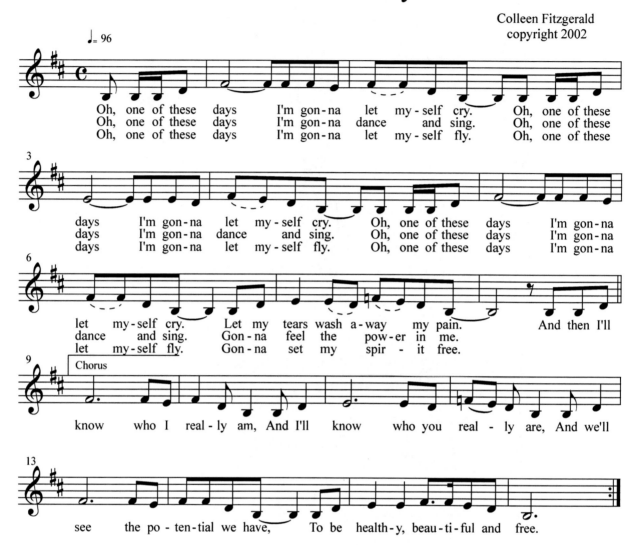

Oh, one of these days I'm gon-na let my-self cry. Oh, one of these
Oh, one of these days I'm gon-na dance and sing. Oh, one of these
Oh, one of these days I'm gon-na let my-self fly. Oh, one of these

days I'm gon-na let my-self cry. Oh, one of these days I'm gon-na
days I'm gon-na dance and sing. Oh, one of these days I'm gon-na
days I'm gon-na let my-self fly. Oh, one of these days I'm gon-na

let my-self cry. Let my tears wash a-way my pain. And then I'll
dance and sing. Gon-na feel the pow-er in me.
let my-self fly. Gon-na set my spir-it free.

Chorus

know who I real-ly am, And I'll know who you real-ly are, And we'll

see the po-ten-tial we have, To be health-y, beau-ti-ful and free.

"One of our women was going through a very difficult time and had to be hospitalized after a suicide attempt. Intuitively, I felt that what she needed more than drugs was to cry, scream, wail, giving voice to her anguish and rage. I could also identify with the need to be more honest about my more painful feelings so that I could freely experience my own power and strength without fear."

Bipolar Blues

Sofia Patience Wilder
copyright 2002

♩= 100 slowly, dramatically

I_ feel too much I_ feel too much I feel

♩= 138 faster, with pep

good I feel bad, feel hap-py feel sad and no-thin' much in be-tween.

I'm up and then down, round and round and I eat a lot of ice

cream. I'm in and I'm out, ov - er and un-der, a roust a-bout or

rent as-sun - der. I get a lot done or I'm lay-in' in my bed,

hap-py as a clam or wish-in' I was dead. This feel-in' too much is too

much to take, You got-ta stay in the mid-dle, girl, for san-it-y's sake!

Healing Has Begun

Linda J Smith Koehler

I am nest-led on the breast of Moth-er Earth,

Bathed in the warmth of Fath-er Sun, Cra-

dled here be - tween the two, I can feel the heal-

ing has be-gun. And I ask the rain to

wash a-way all hat-red, And I ask the wind to

sweep a-way all fear, And I ask the Spir - it of

Love to en - ter ev' - ry heart so that

we will live in peace, so that we will live in peace.

My Spirit Lives On

Linda J. Smith Koehler
Copyright 1996
For Kathleen Lockard

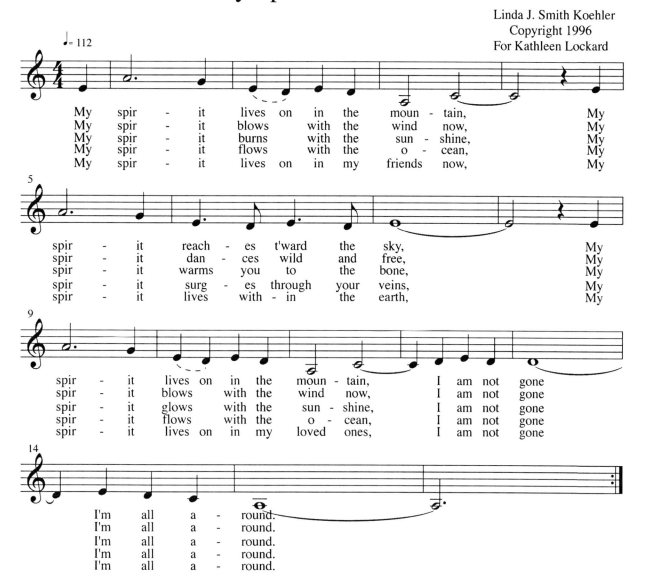

My spir - it lives on in the moun - tain, My
My spir - it blows with the wind now, My
My spir - it burns with the sun - shine, My
My spir - it flows with the o - cean, My
My spir - it lives on in my friends now, My

spir - it reach - es t'ward the sky, My
spir - it dan - ces wild and free, My
spir - it warms you to the bone, My
spir - it surg - es through your veins, My
spir - it lives with - in the earth, My

spir - it lives on in the moun - tain, I am not gone
spir - it blows with the wind now, I am not gone
spir - it glows with the sun - shine, I am not gone
spir - it flows with the o - cean, I am not gone
spir - it lives on in my loved ones, I am not gone

I'm all a - round.
I'm all a - round.
I'm all a - round.
I'm all a - round.
I'm all a - round.

"In 1994 my family moved to Central Pennsylvania for a year and a half. I missed singing with Wings so much that I felt the need to start a group there. Kathleen Lockard became a dear friend and helped me start the group. It was small but the members were enthusiastic and we all became good friends. Kathleen had been living with breast cancer since before I met her. Soon after my family had moved back to Maine, I got a call from her mother saying that I should come back, quickly. I arrived and spent that evening with her. During that night she died at age of thirty-four. I spent the rest of the week with her family and friends, planning and holding a celebration of her life. The day after her memorial service, one friend's car broke down so I drove the forty minutes to pick her up. As I drove through a gap in the rolling mountains, the first verse of the song came to me. As I drove through the valley and along the lake, the rest of the verses came. I arrived at my friend's house and she had popped out for a moment. She was out long enough for me to sit at her piano and write down the tune and words I had come up with. That is how my first song was born."

65

Let Us Hold You Close

Colleen Fitzgerald
copyright 2002

1.Let us hold you close, now. Let us share your pain.
2.Please know that we love you. Please know that we care.

We will give you cour-age 'til you feel strong a - gain. We are your sis-ters and we
Bur-dens that you car - ry are light - er when you share.

care a-bout you. We've known our share of pain and sor-row too.

"We encourage women to bring their sorrows and grief to the healing portion of our singing circle. When Judith told us of her mother's recent death, we were supportive but did not seem to have an appropriate chant with which to comfort her as she cried. I asked the Universe for help and this is the gift I received. My vision is to surround the suffering woman in small, concentric circles and sing to her softly and gently until her grief and pain begin to ease and she regains a sense of her strength and knows that she is not alone. "

Lullaby For A Troubled Spirit

Maryann Ingalls
copyright 2002

Hush, hush, don't you wor-ry now. Hush, hush, don't you wor-ry now.

All is for-giv-en; all is made right. All roads bring bles - sing.

All roads lead home. Hush, hush, don't you wor-ry now. Hush, hush,

don't you wor-ry now. All is for-giv - en; all is made right.

All roads bring bles - sing. All roads lead home Hush, hush, hush.

"Some have come to appreciate this song as one to facilitate a dying person's journey out of this world and into the next. I intended it as a comfort to anyone suffering from grief or remorse. I wrote this on an Ash Wednesday, the beginning of a time which represents for me a special opportunity to return to the divine, a time to remember there are no obstacles to the return, only doorways."

Mother May Your Child Be Healed

Pam Healy
copyright 2002

Moth-er may your child be healed. Moth-er may your child be

healed. Let your peace sur-round her, Let your love em-brace her,

Let your light flow through her, Moth-er may your child be healed.

Moth-er may your child be healed.

"This song came because a friend was sick, as a healing song for women and men and children. The Goddess has given me a great gift – the song comes from Her."

Powers Of The Universe

Linda J Smith Koehler
Copyright 1998

We call the lov - ing pow - ers of the u - ni - verse, and

ask you to make us whole. We call the lov - ing pow - ers of the

u - ni - verse, heal our bo - dies heal our minds heal our souls.

"I was driving to the annual Unitarian Universalist Women's Retreat at Hersey Retreat (the same event at which Women With Wings was conceived a few years earlier.) The theme of the retreat was healing. We knew a few healing songs but I felt inspired to create a new one for our ritual. We sang this song for over an hour and had a powerful experience. I added the word 'loving' a few years later when it was suggested that the song gave too open an invitation."

Chant To Brigit

Kay Gardner
copyright 2002

"In 1995, driving on my way to Wings just after having been diagnosed with uterine cancer, this song came to me. It was Candelmas, or Imbolc, the pagan holy day dedicated to that Celtic Goddess, Brigit. As she is known as a goddess of healing, I felt that she'd visited me just when I needed her. I told everyone what was going on and asked that they pray for my health.

"The next week, the group did an hour-long singing healing circle for me. I laid on a pallet in the middle of the circle. The lights were lowered after flowers and candles were placed around me, and then my sisters surrounded me with song. First they asked me to sing words about how I was feeling, my emotions about my dis-ease, my hopes for my healing. I began, and they each took my words and wove them into a group healing improvisation of joy and affirmation, after which they sang every healing song in our repertoire while women did hands-on healing work for me. It was incredibly powerful.

"After my hysterectomy, I was told by the surgeon that she had excised all of the cancer, that it had been totally contained in my uterus, and that I wouldn't need radiation or chemotherapy. She told me I was 'cured.' Since I'd had symptoms for over a year, this was wonderful news. I feel it was a miracle mediated by Brigit and my singing sisters."

Rainbow Song

Lise Herold
copyright 2002

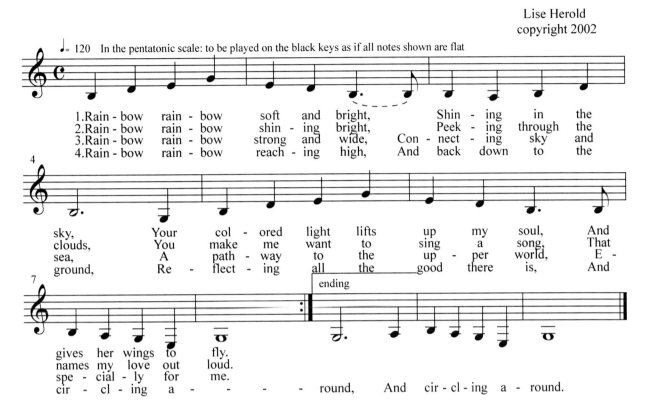

1. Rain - bow rain - bow soft and bright, Shin - ing in the
2. Rain - bow rain - bow shin - ing bright, Peek - ing through the
3. Rain - bow rain - bow strong and wide, Con - nect - ing sky and
4. Rain - bow rain - bow reach - ing high, And back down to the

sky, Your col - ored light lifts up my soul, And
clouds, You make me want to sing a song, That
sea, A path - way to the up - per world, E -
ground, Re - flect - ing all the good there is, And

ending

gives her wings to fly.
names my love out loud.
spe - cial - ly for me.
cir - cl - ing a - - - - round, And cir - cl - ing a - round.

"This song was truly a gift from Spirit. First came the rainbow, while I was driving along in my car, singing sounds but not words. I could hear the sound of someone singing, the words were there and I realized that it was my voice, but it was coming from someone or somewhere else, through me. The person who gifted me this song from spirit is Linda Crane, a woman whom I never met while she had a physical body, but who has a strong connection to song, light, and color, as well as to two very important mutual friends."

Holy Well

Kay Gardner
copyright 2002

May the Moth - er heal the earth, May the Moth - er heal our souls, May Her
wat - ers cleanse the wear - y, May Her wat - ers heal us all.

"In 1998 I co-led a women's mysteries tour of England and Ireland. We visited stone circles and holy wells. This chant came to me after hiking to the Madron Well in Cornwell."

Self, You Are Forgiven

Jami Cass
copyright 2002

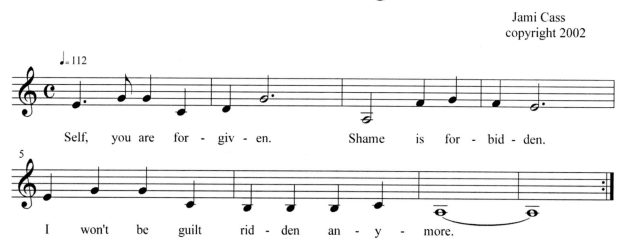

Self, you are for - giv - en. Shame is for - bid - den.
I won't be guilt rid - den an - y - more.

Have Mercy

Rose Iuro-Damon
copyright 2002

"During a heart-to-heart talk with a dear friend, she told me to have mercy on myself. Soon after, this song was born. I envision beginning this song very slowly, then layering in more voices and harmonies, moving into a high-spirited gospel-like feel."

Louise M. Shorette

Songs for Rituals

Dance + Sing back the light

Gentle Blessings in Her name!

Eight times a year the great wheel turns. Eight times a year a sabbat is called. Eight times a year the circle gathers to honor a specific season in its time. Ancient rituals of seasonal recognition are brought into the present. Celtic, pagan, and Wiccan rituals and traditions honor earth, air, fire, and water. We build an altar in the center of the circle and create, with intent, a sacred space for singing. There is always intent to be in harmony with nature and her cycles.

Chant To Call Directions

Kay Gardner
copyright 2002

I call u-pon the pow-ers of the East, of the air and the ris-ing Sun and

Moon, I call up-on the pow-ers of the East, of the air and of new be-

gin - nings. I call u-pon the pow-ers of the South, of the

fire of pas - sion and of will, I call up-on the pow-ers of the

South, of the fire of pas - sion and ful - fill - ment. I

call up-on the pow-ers of the West, of the wat - ers flow and our e-

mo - tions, I call up-on the pow-ers of the West, of the

wat - ers flow and trans-for - ma - tion. I call up-on the pow-ers of the

"As a priestess, I was asked to call the directions at a local interfaith religious service, and though I knew a few longer songs that would have been appropriate, I wanted to create original chants."

We Are Building An Altar

Maryann Ingalls
copyright 2002

We are build-ing an al-tar and we are the stone. We

bring to this cir - cle the gift of our song. We are

build - ing an al - tar and we are the stone. We

bring to this cir - cle the gift of our song.

"This chant is what Women With Wings is all about for me."

The Elements

Pam Healy
copyright 2002

Air, fi - re, water, earth, el - e - ments with us from our birth, yes

Air, fi - re, water, earth, el - e - ments with us from our birth,

Air is the breath of life, The pas - sion for life is fire,

Wat - er be - gins our life, And earth grows the food for life,

Air, fi - re, water, earth, el - e - ments with us from our birth,

Air, fi - re, water, earth, el - e - ments with us from our birth, yes

Air, fi - re, wat - er, earth, el - e - ments with us from our birth.

"A lot of inspiration for the songs comes from the ocean during a walk on the beach.
The Goddess has given me a great gift – the song comes from Her."

Energy Rising

Linda J Smith Koehler
Copyright 1998

I can feel the en - er - gy ris - ing, oh_
I can hear the an - ces-tors sing - ing, oh_

I can feel the el - e - ments swirl - ing, oh_
I can see the spir - its danc - ing, oh_

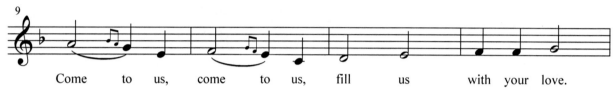

Come to us, come to us, fill us with your love.

Come to us, come to us, be here now.

"This actually started as the wood stove song: 'I can feel the temperature rising…' after I lit my stove for the first time one frosty fall evening. I liked the tune so I kept it in the back of my mind, waiting for the right words. One Thursday night at Wings we raised some wonderful energy, which inspired the words that fit well with the tune."

For Libby

Ina
copyright 2002

♩= 144

I am made of wat - er, from the o - cean I am birthed. The

bones of my an - ces - ters walk with me, for I'm made up of the earth. The

I am air and I can fly high and whis - per through the trees. The

fire that burns down deep in my soul, makes me sing out Bless - ed Be!

Bless - ed Be! Bless - ed Be! The

wat - er and the earth and the air and the fire make me sing out Bless - ed Be!

"This song is dedicated to Libby Roderick because a line in one of her songs was the spark that ignited this one."

Twelve Circles Around The Sun

(Emma's Song)

Rose Iuro-Damon
copyright 2002

1.Twelve cir-cles a - round the sun, I hope you have had plen-ty of fun,

you'll taste joy and you'll taste your tears, as you em-bark on your thir-teenth year.

Grow proud-ly grow up strong, sing your name loud - ly for you are the one.

Grow proud-ly grow up strong, sing your name loud - ly for you are the one.

2.Twelve cir-cles a - round the moon, From babe to child, now a young wo-man soon,

So man-y chang-es are hap-pen-ing here, And man-y more be-fore the end of the year.

Grow proud-ly grow up strong, sing your name loud - ly for you are the one.

Grow proud-ly grow up strong, sing your name loud - ly for you are the one.

"This song was inspired by my youngest daughter's 12th birthday. Though we deal with the frustrations of emerging adolescence, I hope this song reflects a bit of how important she is to me and my hopes for her to grow up strong and proud!"

Come To Me

Mida Ballard
copyright 2002

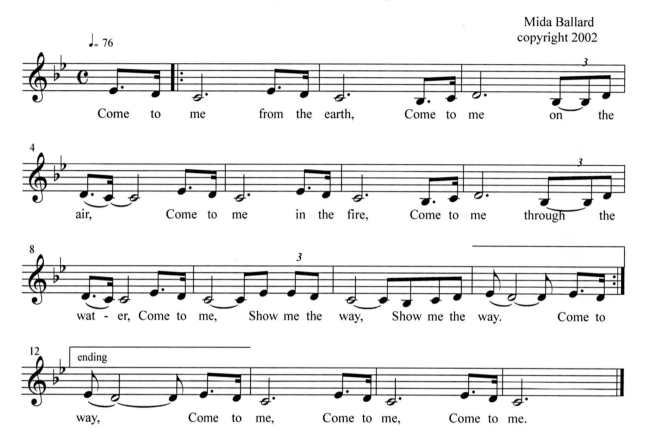

"One night at Wings we were making music with our voices – not a song, just sounds and tones. I heard myself singing the words 'come to me' then a few moments later the words 'show me the way' were added. As I drove home that night singing those words over and over, the rest of the song birthed forth before I had gone four blocks. Before I started going to Wings, I couldn't carry a tune never mind write a song. That night I couldn't have kept that song from coming out if I had tried. It's amazing what can happen when Spirit takes hold in that safe and spiritual environment we call Women With Wings."

Seven Directions

Ina
copyright 2002

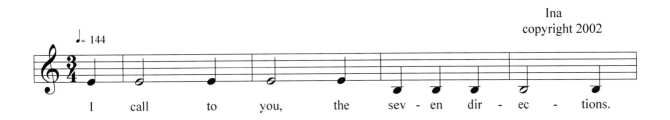

I call to you, the sev - en dir - ec - tions.

Come in - to me. I call to you, the

sev - en dir - ec - tions. Come in - to me.

NORTH

FATHER SKY

WEST   ALL MY RELATIONS   EAST

MOTHER EARTH

SOUTH

Center Chant

Kay Gardner &
Colleen Fitzgerald
copyright 2002

On this night I(we) call the cen - ter, Up from earth and down from sky. En - er - gy meets in the heart of the cen - ter. God - dess and God bring re - new - al and Life.

"Kay and I thought it would be fun to write chants together. This is her melody. I helped with the words."

Candle Magic

Kay Gardner &
Caitlin Matthews
copyright 2002

♩= 108

Moon - beam,   life - dream,   can - dle   shin - ing,   star - gleam

danc - ing in the   night.   Heart's - scheme,   soul's - stream   now   com - bin - ing,

burn   un - flick - er - ing   ho - ly   light.

"Women With Wings was to have a Halloween concert, and we were going to decorate the performance space with candles. Because her Irish bardic poems never fail to inspire me, I looked through Caitlin Matthews' The Celtic Devotional for some words to set to music. These were just right."

Surrender

Ina
copyright 2002

I step in - to the flow, then I let go. I o - pen my mind, my

heart and my soul. I step in - to the flow, then I let go. I

o - pen my mind, my heart and my soul. I sur - ren - der I sur -

ren - der Oh, I sur - ren - der. I o - pen my mind, my

heart and my soul. I o - pen my mind, my heart, and my soul.

Sing

Ina
copyright 2002

Hey! Ev - 'ry - bo - dy come on and sing, If you think you can't well just

look and see. We step in - to the cir - cle and we join our hands,

let - ting go of all of life's de - mands. We o - pen our mouths and we

o - pen our hearts, Mak - ing mu - sic from the mo - ment we start. We

drum and we rat - tle and the rhy - thm takes hold, We sing and we dance and we

o - pen our souls. So come on in and let your voice be heard, Our

mu - sic goes out and heals the world. Our mu - sic goes out and heals the world.

Winter Solstice

Linda J Smith Koehler
Copyright 1999

Win - ter Sol - stice, time of dark and cold - ness,

Close your eyes and search with-in, to tap the source where you be-gin.

Win - ter Sol - stice, time of dark and cold - ness,

In the still - ness of the night, look with-in to find your light.

Win - ter Sol - stice, time of dark and cold - ness,

Bur - row deep with - in your soul, to find the things that make you whole.

"This tune first came to me in the fall of 1999 when I was singing a friend's name playfully to her. In December I found the words to fit the tune and express my thoughts on what the dark time of year can be for."

Jump The Fire

Linda J Smith Koehler
Copyright 2000

Jump the fi - re,   dance wild and   free   to - night.   Jump the

fi - re,   make love with   me   to - night.   Jump the fi - re,   as the

leaves   burst free.   Jump the   fi - re, Jump the fi - re,   with me.

"Ahh May! What more can I say?"

Our Hearts Are Open

Rose Iuro-Damon
copyright 2002

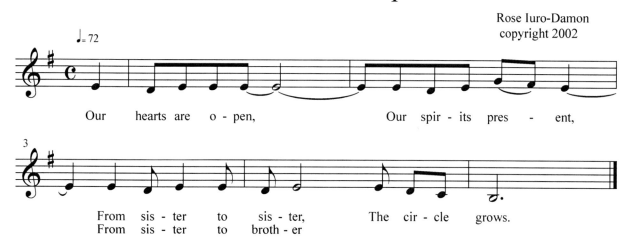

Our   hearts are o - pen,   Our   spir - its pres - ent,

From   sis - ter   to   sis - ter,   The   cir - cle   grows.
From   sis - ter   to   broth - er

"Several women on Mt. Desert Island used to gather for monthly Moon Sister Circles. This song was spontaneously born on one of those nights. It just rose within me and I sang it. Of all my songs, this one has never changed at all from that night!"

A Woman In The Tribe Has Died

Robin Fre

A wo-man in the tribe has died. A wo-man in the tribe has died.

Each wo-man com-forts each wo-man com-forts each wo-man com-forts each.

The first time we sang this song for one of our own members was at our
Thursday circle the night after Kay passed. Over 60 wingers were present.

We Release You

Linda J Smith Koehler
Copyright 1999

Wo_ spir-its, we re-lease you and we send you on your way.
or: Wo_ spir-its, we em-brace you and we're glad you came our way.

Wo_ spir-its, we thank you for all your help on this fine day.
Wo_ spir-its, we thank you for all your help on this fine day.

"I wrote this in the shower after a discussion about the need to release all that we call."

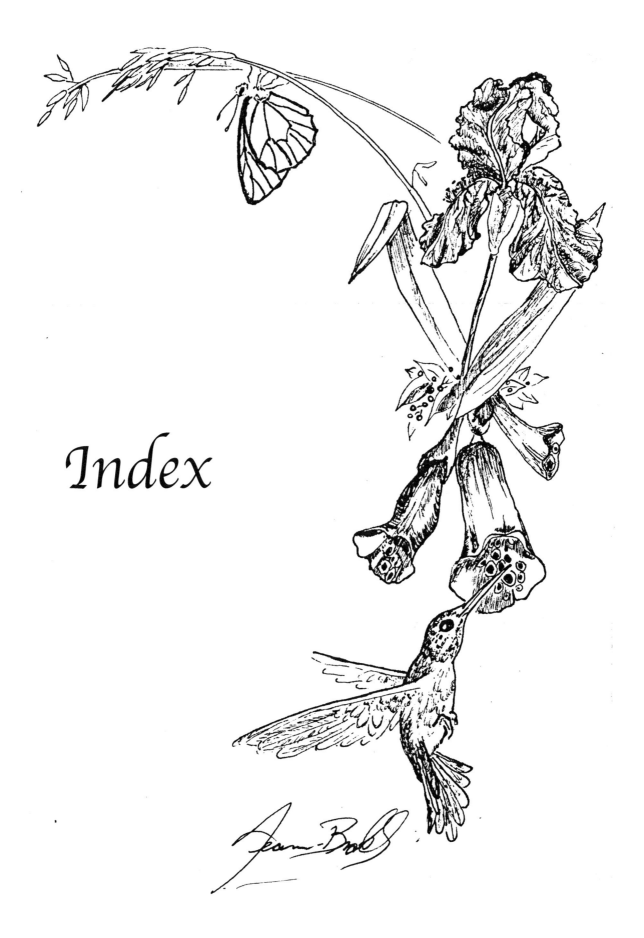

Index

Index of Songs by Title and Category
A - Affirmations, E – Mother Earth, G – Goddess,
H – Healing, M – Moon, R - Rituals

As you sing our songs, may you be inspired to create your own songs.

Hand in Hand and Heart to Heart

Home to the River of Love

may the blessings of love rest upon you

may love's peace abide with you

May love's presence illuminate your life

Now and forever more.

HAND IN HAND & HEART TO HEART
Original Chants and Songs of
Affirmation and Empowerment

Twenty of the songs in this songbook have been recorded by
Women With Wings and are available on the Hand in Hand
& Heart to Heart CD from:

Ladyslipper, Inc.,
PO Box 3124, Durham, NC 27715 USA,
1-800-634-6044, orders@ladyslipper.org

*"Women With Wings' Hand in Hand & Heart to Heart is a beautiful, well-produced
CD of 20 uplifting, healing, and empowering original songs and chants by many women.
Over 40 voices sing a capella, in unison or with simple harmony and drum accompani-
ment, offering us a rich selection of easy to learn words and music. It is a wonderful
resource, especially for women's circles and rituals."*

Kate Marks, therapist, sound healer, author of
Circle of Song: Songs, Chants and Dances for Ritual and Celebration

All 20 songs from the CD included in this Songbook

Breinigsville, PA USA
26 April 2010
236788BV00002B/1/P